*"Writing is a dog's life,
but the only life worth living."*

—GUSTAVE FLAUBERT, FRENCH WRITER

Calliope and Thalia, two of the Muses, the goddesses of literary inspiration

Lives of the

Writers

COMEDIES, TRAGEDIES
(and What the Neighbors Thought)

WRITTEN BY **Kathleen Krull**

ILLUSTRATED BY **Kathryn Hewitt**

sandpiper

Houghton Mifflin Harcourt

Boston   New York

I am indebted to Sister Della, O.S.F. (Marie Tollstrup);
Sister Jean Bernard, O.P.; professors in the English department of
Lawrence University; and to the collections of literary biographies
at the Athenaeum Music and Arts Library of La Jolla,
the University of California, San Diego, Library, and the San Diego Public Library.
— K.K.

Text copyright © 1994 by Kathleen Krull
Illustrations copyright © 1994 by Kathryn Hewitt

The Library of Congress has cataloged the hardcover edition as follows:
Krull, Kathleen.
Lives of the writers: comedies, tragedies (and what the neighbors thought)/written by Kathleen Krull;
illustrated by Kathryn Hewitt.—1st ed.
p. cm.
Summary: The lives of twenty writers, ranging from Dickens, the Brontës, and Poe to Twain,
Sandburg, and Langston Hughes, are profiled in this eclectic, humorous, and informative collection.
Includes bibliographical references and index.
I. Authors—Juvenile literature. [I. Authors.] I. Hewitt, Kathryn, ill. II. Title.
PN452.K75 1994
[B]—dc20 93-32436

ISBN 978-0-15-248009-7 hardcover
ISBN 978-0-15-204606-4 paperback

Manufactured in China
LEO 10 9 8 7 6 5 4

4500292426

To Susan Cohen, friend of writers

—K. K.

To Pam Moore, artist and sister extraordinaire

—K. H.

CONTENTS

$\mathcal{I}$NTRODUCTION

YOU MIGHT THINK that writers—even famous ones—lead quiet, mousy lives. Perhaps they spend their days with only the modest tools of their trade for company, piping up now and then to plead for more money.

Allow the neighbors to disagree. After all, a typewriter does keep the neighborhood on edge when it clatters fifteen hours a day (as with Jack London), and neighbors are the first to notice when a writer (such as Langston Hughes) keeps odd hours. Neighbors have been jarred awake by temper tantrums when a writer's shirts lack buttons (Twain). They've partaken of a novelist's lavish Polynesian feasts (Stevenson) and of a poet's fresh gingerbread lowered out the window in a basket (Dickinson). Where neighbors are concerned, writers have provoked storms of gossip (Dickens), endless curiosity (Austen), tears from small children (Alcott), and accusations of murder (Cervantes).

Some writers live simply and quietly (Singer), while some live noisily and like to carry a gun (Hurston). But the writers in this book, representing different countries, time periods, and literary forms and styles, do have things in common. About their writing, they had a persistence that led not only to success—sometimes during their lifetimes, sometimes not—but also to eccentricities, some amusing, some tragic.

And their work itself was rarely quiet. It was blamed for outbreaks of plague (Shakespeare), inspired fashion for an entire generation (Burnett), and created overnight fame (Poe). It was condemned as "dangerous" (White), not to mention "wicked" (Charlotte Brontë) and "demonic" (Emily Brontë). Sometimes it required a secret existence (Alcott); sometimes it was featured on every TV talk show from "Today" to "Tonight" (Sandburg).

All of these writers have works that are still passionately read. The writing, above all, is why we remember these poets, playwrights, and novelists today.

Here, escorted by the Muses, the guiding spirits of writers, are the lives of twenty writers, in all their comedy and tragedy. These most unquiet stories, never before collected in one volume, are offered now as a way of getting closer to the writers—and their writings.

—Kathleen Krull

RICE CAKES AND MOONLIGHT
MURASAKI SHIKIBU

BORN IN KYOTO, JAPAN, 973?
DIED IN KYOTO, JAPAN, 1025?

Japanese writer famous for The Tale of Genji,
*sometimes considered the world's oldest novel and a
major influence on Japanese literature*

MURASAKI SHIKIBU EXCELLED at her studies. "Just my luck," her father would sigh. "If only you were a boy — how proud I would be." But he did not stop her education, even though it was an era when scholarly girls were looked down upon. Murasaki took to concealing some of her learning, such as her ability to write and read in Chinese — considered then to be impossible tasks for women.

At about age twenty-five, she married and had a daughter. After her husband died two years later, Murasaki spent several anxious years not knowing what her future would hold. Her one desire, as a widow, was to be inconspicuous, to avoid any behavior that might give people cause for gossip. She would sit for hours by the window, watching a flower open in the moonlight, making notes for a novel.

Then her father arranged to have Murasaki appointed as a lady-in-waiting to the teenage Empress Shoshi. Murasaki had few duties around the palace, leaving her plenty of time to continue her writing.

Life at court was cut off from the rest of the world. People spent their time with superficial poetry, music, romance, and gossip. Women in particular were kept secluded. Shoshi's court was more strict than most — when men were around, for example, women had to hide themselves behind screens. Murasaki would have preferred another court, where ladies were "always off to see the fading of the moon at dawn," as she wrote in her secret diary.

Murasaki also disliked the attention of Shoshi's father, the minister of state. He would hand her plum blossoms over the top of her screen, putting her in the uncomfortable position of having to write him thank-you poems. Like others in court, he made fun of the serious novel she was writing.

Shoshi wanted to learn Chinese, a desire that was shocking in her society. Word leaked out that Murasaki knew Chinese, and in exchange for teaching her, Shoshi gave Murasaki presents of paper (rare at the time), brushes, and ink.

Murasaki was considered quiet, melancholy, even pretentious. She liked to live "buried in my own thoughts like a tree stump in the earth." Poetry was a court social activity, but she stayed out of the competitions. She imagined that others thought her a monster, while she thought of herself as kind and gentle.

Murasaki did enjoy the complexities of court clothing. Women wore many layers of gauze robes, and the color combinations of the sleeves had certain meanings. The meanings are lost today, but we know that Murasaki followed the rules of fashion. She might wear a jacket with cuffs of white lined with pale green over one robe of red lined with purple, and another of pale green lined with dark green.

Otherwise, Murasaki lived simply. She ate rice cakes and kept her room warm by burning charcoal in a hibachi. She owned two stringed instruments, called *kotos,* on which she played sad music in the evenings. In her room were two cupboards full of poems, tales, and Chinese books that she looked at when she felt lonely. Sometimes she destroyed old letters and papers by burning them or by using them to make dollhouses. She thought for a while of becoming a Buddhist nun.

Looking at the moon was thought dangerous for women; it was said to cause premature aging, and older women were treated harshly in this society. But

Murasaki found ways to keep watching the moon and took to calling herself a decrepit old fossil. It is believed that she was fifty-two when she died.

Her daughter, Kenshi, also wrote poetry and had many poems chosen for royal collections. She rose to the position of principal handmaid and may have lived until she was eighty-four.

ℬOOKMARKS

➥ Amid the brilliant but frivolous court society, Murasaki disliked the rudeness of the men around her—none of them were like the hero of her novel, Prince Genji (the "Shining One"). In *The Tale of Genji,* a chronicle of the career of the prince and the women he was associated with, Murasaki used writing techniques that did not appear in Western literature for centuries. She depicted human emotions and changes in nature in ways never seen before and influential ever since.

➥ The heroine in *The Tale of Genji* is named Murasaki; this was not a case of the author naming a character after herself. Rather, the name by which she is now known combined a title of her father's (Shikibu) and the name of the heroine she created. Murasaki Shikibu's real name, like those of most Japanese women of that time, is unknown.

MIGUEL DE CERVANTES

BORN IN ALCALÁ DE HENARES, SPAIN, 1547
DIED IN MADRID, SPAIN, 1616

*Spanish poet and novelist considered by many as the
father of the modern novel, most famous for*
Don Quixote of La Mancha

IN 1569 A MAN thought to be Miguel de Cervantes was arrested for fighting a duel. At that time, this was a serious offense, punished by getting one's right hand cut off in public.

But Cervantes escaped—and sneaked out of Spain to join its army in Italy. There, though he had saved his right hand, he lost the use of his left hand when it was shattered by a gunshot.

Undeterred, he decided to make the military his career and asked some prominent people to write letters to the king recommending a promotion to captain. He was returning to Madrid with this petition when fresh disaster struck. Barbary pirates captured his ship, took everyone prisoner, and held them for ransom in Algiers in North Africa, the most notorious pirate city of the times.

Cervantes, unfortunately, was still carrying those letters of recommendation. The pirates thus thought he was much more important than he actually was, and set an impossibly high ransom. It took Cervantes's family five years to come up with the money.

So Cervantes spent five years in slavery . . . playing cards, seeing how much higher he could jump in his chains than the other prisoners could, writing poetry, scavenging food, and planning escape. Four times he made daring escape attempts—and four times he failed. He gained a reputation as a courageous rebel, hardy and determined amid appalling cruelty and hopelessness.

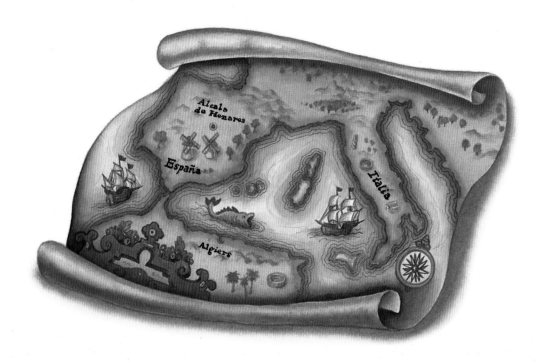

Freed from slavery and back in Spain at last, Cervantes had nothing to show for his military career except a maimed hand and a pile of debts. He went to work collecting supplies for Spain's army—a job guaranteed to make the collector unpopular. He managed to get himself excommunicated (kicked out of the Catholic church) not once but twice, for collecting supplies too efficiently from resentful church officials. He also spent seven months in jail after being falsely accused of stealing supplies.

"I content myself with little, although I deserve much," Cervantes wrote. Always poor, he moved often, and even when he had a little money he was known as a "soft touch" — he would give his money away.

Cervantes and his wife, Catalina, had no children. In fact, they often lived apart, and Cervantes had two children with other women. His family life, when he had one, was not always smooth. Once he and his relatives were thrown in jail after neighbors wrongly accused them of involvement in a local murder.

Although Cervantes knew that he was "better versed in misfortunes than in verses," he settled down to write feverishly for the last sixteen years of his life. *Don Quixote of La Mancha* and other works made him famous, but he was more popular outside Spain than in his own country. He never escaped poverty.

Cervantes had a lifelong stutter, bad teeth, and arthritis. He died of diabetes at age sixty-nine.

His will left everything he had — which was only the profits from his last book — to Catalina, and it's thought that his publisher cheated her out of the money.

$\mathscr{B}$OOKMARKS

➥ After Cervantes wrote part one of *The Ingenious Hidalgo Don Quixote of La Mancha*, about the mishaps of a chivalrous country gentleman, ten years passed before he wrote part two. He might never have finished the novel at all — he liked some of his other works better — had not another writer enraged him by publishing his own part two to *Don Quixote*.

➥ Many people today know *Don Quixote* by way of the modern musical *Man of La Mancha* (most famous for its theme song, "The Impossible Dream"), which is based on Cervantes's novel.

"CURST BE HE THAT MOVES MY BONES"

WILLIAM SHAKESPEARE

BORN IN 1564 AND DIED IN 1616
IN STRATFORD-ON-AVON, ENGLAND

*English poet and playwright, famous for
comedies, tragedies, historical plays, and sonnets;
the most well-known author in English literature*

A MAN WHO KNEW William Shakespeare well called him open, honest, and free. But for someone who didn't mean to be mysterious, he left plenty of mysteries behind.

We know that Stratford, where he grew up, was a magnet for fairs and traveling entertainers, who would perform plays about such characters as Robin Hood and his Merry Men. We also know that grammar schools of the time were demanding (nine hours of studies a day, with no vacations), and so Shakespeare probably got used to working hard.

The first thing on record about Shakespeare is his marriage at age eighteen to Anne Hathaway, a farmer's daughter eight years older than he was. Their daughter Susanna was born six months later. Before he turned twenty-one, Shakespeare also had twins, Judith and Hamnet.

After this come "the lost years," a period for which we know virtually nothing about what Shakespeare was doing. From the breadth of knowledge evident in his plays, he could have been working as anything from a butcher to a law clerk, from

19

a schoolmaster to a gardener. He could have assisted his father (a glove-maker and trader in commodities), or taken a job in publishing, or been a soldier. He seemed both an outdoors kind of person, with a broad knowledge of nature and sports, and a well-read indoors person. There is a story that he was caught poaching a nobleman's deer and was forced to leave Stratford.

Shakespeare next surfaced as an actor in London, and it's known that some people were jealous of him for his ability to write plays as well as act. He was on his way to becoming a true man of the theater: actor, playwright, producer, and theater owner.

It is thought that Shakespeare was not a particularly strong actor. But his premature baldness gave him a distinguished appearance, and it's believed that he played the ghost in *Hamlet* and various "kingly" roles. He often wrote parts specifically for the actors he knew would play them. His favorite actor, apparently, was Richard Burbage, the original portrayer of many of Shakespeare's greatest roles, including Hamlet, King Lear, Othello, and Richard III.

Because he was producing two plays each year — thirty-eight plays in all — it is believed that Shakespeare wrote rapidly. He probably used a quill pen made from goose feathers. His fellow actors bragged that Shakespeare "never blotted a line," meaning that he rarely made revisions once he had something down on paper. He was involved in every aspect of his plays and was able to see exactly what worked on stage (and what didn't). The large, restless audiences worked hard for the pennies that bought tickets, and if they were bored, they could turn a play into a circus.

In London, Shakespeare rented rooms or lived with friends, arrangements that left more time for his writing. Meanwhile, his wife stayed in Stratford. Shakespeare visited her only about once a year. Do their separate lives mean their marriage was unhappy? We will never know. Perhaps Mrs. Shakespeare disapproved of the theater. (Many people did — some even thought the much-dreaded plague was God's punishment for theater.)

So Shakespeare spent his time with the other actors, rehearsing (in the mornings), performing (in the afternoons and evenings), touring, eating together, looking out for each other. He took no vacations, and it's thought that he never toured outside England.

Outbreaks of the plague occasionally closed down everything in London. When theaters were closed (and no new plays were needed), Shakespeare wrote poetry, including 154 sonnets. Thousands of articles have been written about the identity of the "Dark Lady," addressed in many of the sonnets, and "Mr. W. H.," addressed in others. Both people remain a complete mystery.

Shakespeare must have loved the theater above all else, for despite the popularity of his poems (which were a more secure route to fame and fortune), he devoted almost all his energy to his plays. His theater group, known first as the Chamberlain's Men and later as the King's Men, was the most successful of its day, a favorite both of Queen Elizabeth I and her successor, King James I. The group's members lived quietly, worked hard, and became wealthy. Shakespeare made almost no money from his writing but instead earned his modest fortune as an actor. He invested shrewdly, mostly in real estate.

Shakespeare's work kept him too busy to do anything wild or get into trouble. He never fought duels, got into debt, or went to jail, and he rarely even held grudges or took offense. He was easygoing, reserved, and tactful. One friend described him as "very good company," with a "ready and pleasant" wit. He did nothing to get his plays published, which may mean his ego wasn't wrapped up in his work. Instead, what seems to have meant the most to him was being recognized as a gentleman. Thus, as soon as he could afford it, he applied for the Shakespeare family coat of arms (a coveted status symbol displayed on one's house or clothes) — a picture of a gold spear with a silver head. This officially made him a "gentleman" and entitled him to be called Master.

Back in Stratford, he bought the second-largest house in town — New Place, a mansion with three stories, ten fireplaces, two barns, and two orchards. He added mulberry trees to the garden and set about doing much-needed work on the house as thriftily as possible. At age forty-six, after writing *The Tempest,* he retired with his wife to tend to New Place and live the life of a country gentleman and good neighbor. He was friends with all the richest citizens — lawyers, land-owners, money lenders. When visiting preachers came to town, they stayed at Shakespeare's home.

Shakespeare died at fifty-two of unknown causes. The rumor that he caught a chill while partying with playwright friends is probably not true.

His will was generous, but — unlike most wills of the time — it showed no private emotion. He left money to colleagues and to the poor; a silver bowl to Judith (Hamnet had died at age eleven); his sword to a lawyer friend; his clothes to his sister Joan; and his silverware to his granddaughter. In his most mysterious provision, he left his "second-best bed" to his wife. The best bed went to Susanna and her husband, John, along with New Place.

His will went to great lengths to make sure that all of his real estate stayed together and went to a single male heir. In this goal he was defeated, as his last direct descendant died some fifty years later and his properties began to be dispersed among strangers.

On his tomb at Holy Trinity Church in Stratford is the Shakespeare coat of arms and a verse that ends: "Blest be the man that spares these stones, / And curst be he that moves my bones."

Bookmarks

- The Globe Theater was the principal home of Shakespeare's acting company and the site of the first performances of such plays as *Hamlet, Macbeth, King Lear,* and *Othello. As You Like It* may have been written for the Globe's opening. During a performance of *Henry VIII,* a cannon set fire to the thatched roof. No one was hurt, though one man's pants caught fire; the person next to him put the fire out with a bottle of beer. The theater was rebuilt (with a tile roof this time) but was torn down eventually, so we don't know precisely what it looked like.
- Although most plays written at that time have not been preserved, Shakespeare's were — by his own King's Men. Seven years after his death, the King's Men published a complete collection of the plays, known as the First Folio.
- Most serious actors consider Shakespeare's work the ultimate test of their skill. Famous Shakespearean actors include Laurence Olivier, Orson Welles, Vanessa Redgrave, Claire Bloom, Richard Burton, John Barrymore, James Earl Jones, Sarah Bernhardt, and — as an amateur player — Charles Dickens.
- So few facts are available about Shakespeare's life that more than four thousand books have been written speculating whether he actually wrote the plays at all. At least fifty-eight other candidates, including Queen Elizabeth I, have been proposed as the real author.

JANE AUSTEN

BORN IN STEVENTON, ENGLAND, 1775
DIED IN WINCHESTER, ENGLAND, 1817

*English novelist famous for witty novels—
including* Pride and Prejudice *and* Emma*—
with intelligent, independent heroines*

GIRLS DURING JANE AUSTEN'S time were told to "sit up straight, hold your shoulders back, don't lounge, don't cross your legs, don't bite your nails, don't pick your nose, and don't blow on your soup."

Austen absorbed all this and in addition became a high-speed reader, spending long hours with books. Although school ended for her at age eleven, she was much more educated than other girls of her day, thanks to her father, a country parson who valued education.

As a teen she loved to dance. One year she wore through four pairs of dancing slippers. Some called her "a husband-hunting butterfly," but although she had several proposals, she never married. She never met a man who appreciated her intelligence and education, and she couldn't bear the idea of marrying just for money. Far better to be single—although single women at the time were often poor.

Austen solved this by never living apart from her family. She led a quiet, domestic life, and her family was the center of her world. She was especially close to her older sister Cassandra; they shared a bedroom. Austen was reserved with strangers, who found her arrogant or even fierce, but her family treated her as an agreeable mouse. None of them thought much about the writing she was always doing; it was just something that kept Jane busy, like the needlework other women did.

But all the while, Austen was watching people (including herself), keeping track of silly behavior. At dinner parties she didn't say much, but the next day she might write a letter about "another stupid party last night," or "I was as civil to them as their bad breath would allow."

As much as she wanted to be a humble sister and obedient daughter, she was also extremely proud of the small sums she earned when her family persuaded her to start publishing her books. She wrote, "If I *am* a wild beast, I cannot help it." And no one had to know it — the title pages of her work read "By a Lady."

Austen got up early and practiced piano. Preparing breakfast was her responsibility (coffee, tea, pound cake, bread and butter, and sometimes chocolate). She spent mornings in the drawing room, writing novels on her lap-size mahogany desk, with a quill pen that constantly needed mending.

Women were considered "interruptable" and had almost no time during the day to call their own. If neighbors came over, Austen foiled their immense curiosity by folding her writing paper in half to cover her work or by acting as if she were just jotting down a shopping list. After lunch she walked in the nearby woods or visited friends. She always wore a cap, and her clothes were never quite in fashion.

Austen was a world-class aunt. From age seventeen on she had a new niece or nephew almost every year, and to them she was a pretty, funny storyteller. Cheerful and energetic, she made paper boats and played catch, cards, and pickup sticks.

Austen died in Cassandra's arms at age forty-one, possibly from cancer or tuberculosis. In her obituaries, she was revealed as the author of six novels. That she would gradually become famous did not occur to anyone then, however, and her gravestone in Winchester Cathedral makes no mention of her writing.

*B*OOKMARKS

➤ Austen liked *Pride and Prejudice* better than any of her other books. It has a famous opening sentence: "It is a truth universally acknowledged, that a single man in possession of a good fortune must be in want of a wife." Its heroine, Elizabeth Bennet, has been called one of the most admired women in English literature; Austen said, "*I* think her as delightful a creature as ever appeared in print."

➤ Austen said that her novel *Emma* was about "a heroine whom no one but myself will much like" — yet *Emma* is considered by many to be her best novel. The Prince of Wales, one of her small group of fans, asked her to dedicate the book to him; although she disliked him, she didn't feel she was in a position to refuse.

➤ Austen was so discreet about her work that even her family didn't always know what she was up to. Once a niece picked up a copy of *Sense and Sensibility* in Austen's presence and quickly threw it down, saying that she could tell it was trash just by reading the title.

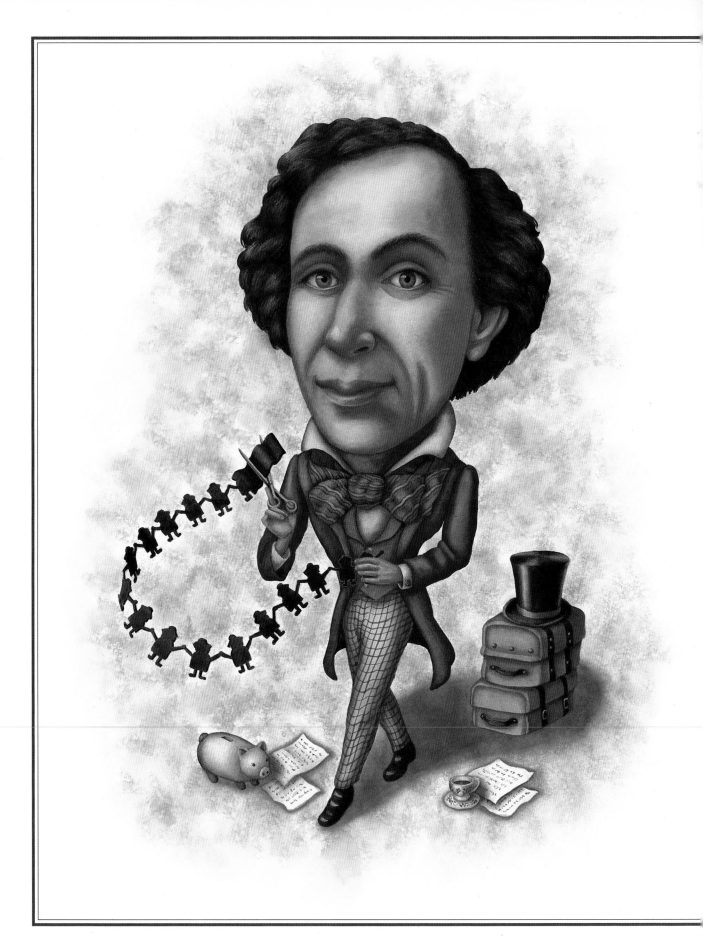

Hans Christian Andersen

BORN IN ODENSE, DENMARK, 1805
DIED IN ROLIGHED, DENMARK, 1875

*Danish writer of fairy tales, including
"The Emperor's New Clothes," "The Steadfast Tin Soldier,"
"Thumbelina," and "The Ugly Duckling"*

"MY LIFE IS A FAIRY TALE," Hans Christian Andersen once wrote, and most people would have agreed: he *was* the ugly duckling.

Awkward and unattractive, Andersen came from the humblest possible background—his family history included crime, illiteracy, insanity, and alcoholism. He spent his lonely childhood playing with puppets and a toy theater. On winter nights (when darkness lasts as long as seventeen hours in Denmark), he heated coins and pressed them against the windows to melt the frost so he could peer at the snowy scenes outside.

He went to work in a tobacco factory at age eleven and then, dreading a lifetime of this, took the money he'd been saving up in a clay pig and left home for Copenhagen. Although he received almost no encouragement, he was convinced that he excelled at singing, dancing, acting, and drawing. "First one has to endure terrible adversity," he assured his mother, "then you become famous."

All his life, the word even his friends used most often to describe Andersen was *childlike*. A nature-lover, he was known to hug trees. He was too anxious to please, too easily intimidated, and a bumbler. Once he got so nervous during an exam that he sprayed the professor's face with ink by mistake. Talkative and eager, he would collar people to read his work to them. Amazingly, people *were* charmed by Andersen and gave him scholarships and opportunities.

He even dressed like a child. Always frugal, he wore clothes and shoes long after he had outgrown them. If someone gave him a coat that was too big, he would stuff it with newspapers to make it fit. He liked to read books while lying on a sofa, wearing brightly colored slippers and a dressing gown.

He had one hobby that appealed to adults and children alike. His huge hands were skilled with a pair of scissors, and he would cut delicate creations from paper as he talked — animals, castles, goblins, and fairies.

Andersen knew he was an ugly duckling ("His nose as mighty as a cannon, / His eyes are tiny, like green peas" was how he put it), but he was vain, too, and he loved to be photographed. He probably would have liked this book (he liked stories about famous people), but he might have wanted the whole book to himself.

Andersen never settled into a home of his own. When in Denmark he stayed in hotels or with friends — he was often designated the family "candle snuffer" because he was so tall. He preferred wandering, and whenever he had enough money he went off traveling. His first train ride (at age thirty-five) was magical; he loved to watch the landscape fly by.

He desperately wanted to get married but never did. The women *he* chose were either long dead (his first true love was a portrait of the ancestor of a friend) or did not return his affection. The women who chose *him* repelled him.

When he was feeling especially melancholy, Andersen would get bad toothaches (even — after he lost all his teeth — in his false teeth). He feared death — from a splinter, food poisoning, murder, or being buried alive. He sometimes put a sign next to his bed that read I AM NOT REALLY DEAD, so that people would know he was just asleep. Most of all he feared dying young, insane, and alone.

He was, in fact, seventy when he died — probably of liver cancer — and by that time he was a much-loved figure around the world.

*B*OOKMARKS

➦ Andersen wrote plays, operas, novels, poetry, and travel books but today is known best for his 168 fairy tales. "The Little Mermaid" was his favorite, and he saw himself in the heroine. He too had come from the sea (the islands of Denmark), and all his life he felt like a "fish out of water," longing to be accepted.

➦ Andersen wrote "The Nightingale" while in love with Jenny Lind, whose nickname was the Swedish Nightingale. Andersen showered Lind — the most famous singer of the day — with flowers, poems, and gifts, but his love was not returned.

➦ A magazine once sent Andersen three woodcuts as the basis for a story. He chose one of a ragged little girl with her apron full of matches and wrote "The Little Match Girl." The woodcut reminded him of his mother, who as a child had been forced to beg.

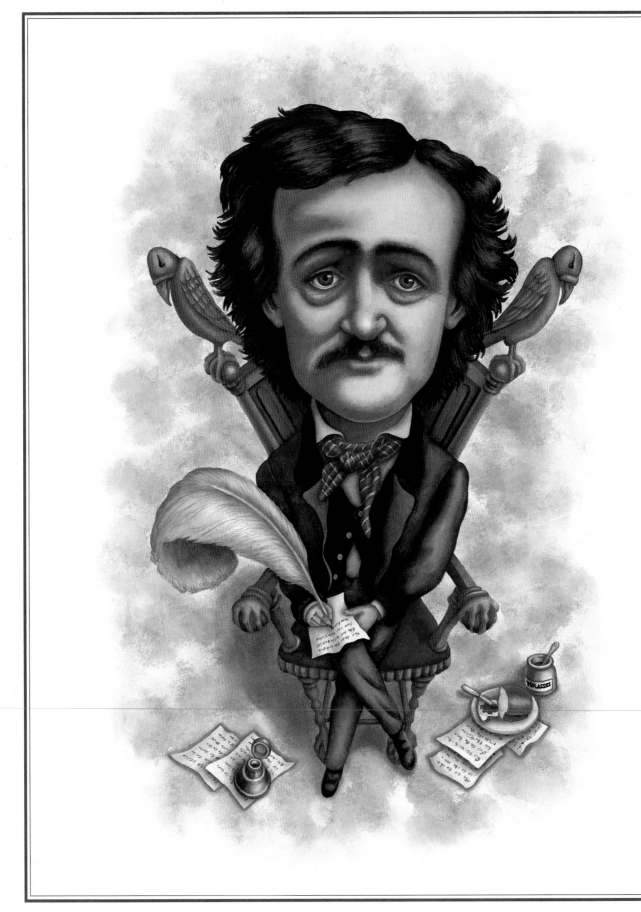

EDGAR ALLAN POE

BORN IN BOSTON, MASSACHUSETTS, 1809
DIED IN BALTIMORE, MARYLAND, 1849

American poet and short story writer,
often considered the creator of both the
detective story and horror fiction

"I HAVE MANY occasional dealings with Adversity," the man born Edgar Poe once said, "but the want of parental affection has been the heaviest of my trials."

Any happiness he ever had seems to have ended when his mother, a popular actress, died at age twenty-four. (Poe's father, a failed actor, had deserted the family.) His mother had little to leave her son but memories and a miniature portrait of herself.

Tobacco merchant John Allan and his wife took two-year-old Edgar into their Virginia home and gave him their name. But they never formally adopted him, which meant he had no official family. In fact, as a consequence of their many quarrels, the Allans refused to have anything to do with Poe once he grew up. (Poe never used the name Allan and always signed his name Edgar A. Poe.)

Poe joined the army for a time, attended West Point for a year, and then went to live with his aunt Maria ("Muddy"). Four years later, at age twenty-seven, Poe married her daughter and his cousin, Virginia ("Sissy"), age thirteen. He called her his darling little wifey. She called him Eddie and adored him.

Muddy and Sissy mothered Poe. The three of them moved often, renting cottages or rooms in boardinghouses. They usually lived on the outskirts of cities. Poe liked to walk in the woods and would go there to escape if they had visitors he didn't like. Lack of money was their constant plague. Sometimes they were so poor they lived on bread and molasses for weeks at a time or went without food altogether. Poe was always in debt; when he once wanted to file for bankruptcy, he couldn't afford the fee to do so. He owned few possessions — just a few books, two pine tables he had built, a cat named Catterina, and tropical birds that he kept in cages. Despite his poverty, Poe made a point of dressing very neatly (if shabbily) and acting the part of the refined southern gentleman.

He worked for various magazines, writing criticism and editing others' work, as much as fifteen hours a day but seldom for more than a year at any one place. Poe was an alcoholic by this time, which often interfered with his work. When he wasn't drinking, he was quiet and disciplined. When he was, he could be abrasive, insulting friends or leaving shops without paying. He would often disappear and be found days later wandering in the woods. People could guess Poe's state of mind by looking at the state of his clothes. If his coat was inside out, that was a bad sign.

Poe worked on his own stories and poems at night. When he was between jobs (sometimes for years at a time), he spent the mornings in his study and the afternoons in his flower garden (he loved flowers). He often recited poetry to Sissy and Muddy, and when he read a moving poem of his own, such as "Annabel Lee," he would cry. He was never paid well for his writing.

Poe was always slim and stayed in good shape by taking long walks. When young he was an outstanding athlete, famous for jumping and swimming. He always tried to be first in whatever he did and boasted for years about the time he swam six miles against a strong tide. A boxer, he would encourage boys to hit him in the chest to show he could take it.

As an adult Poe fought the world. His behavior was sometimes so bizarre that many thought he was insane or committing a slow suicide. He was notorious for writing cruel reviews, using words like *sickening* and *worthless* to describe almost every writer of the day. Or the reviews might be just the opposite — it was as if he were writing as two entirely different people, one full of hate and the other full of love. Sometimes he perversely acted against his own professional interests and feuded with people who could have helped him. He attacked other writers for plagiarism and grammatical errors — the same sins he was occasionally guilty of himself.

He also got into real fights; the scar near his left eye was caused by the ring of a man who punched him (and who had called him Marmaduke Hammerhead in print). He criticized whole literary communities — of writers in Boston he said, "Their pumpkin pies are delicious. Their poetry is not so good." He suspected people of plotting against him (and because he made so many enemies, they sometimes were). Sooner or later, Poe antagonized almost everyone in his life except

Sissy and Muddy, with whom he was always gentle. The only well-known writer he never attacked was Charles Dickens.

Poe usually looked pained, as if nightmares and visions haunted him. He always dressed in black, even in summer heat. Few people ever saw Poe smile; he didn't have much of a sense of humor. Sometimes, to earn a little money, he wrote jokes for magazines — "Why is a bleeding cat like a question? Because it's a catty gory [category]" — but they usually weren't very funny.

Poe often begged friends and neighbors for money. When he had it, he spent it on Sissy's education or on gifts (including a piano and harp) for her. Once he spent hundreds of dollars on tables and chairs before he saw the new house they had rented, which turned out to be too tiny for the furniture. On a tour to raise money for a magazine he badly wanted to start up, he managed to lose his trunk of clothes, the notes for the lectures he was to give, and one of his shoes. Once he had attained his lifelong goal of running his own magazine, it lasted only five weeks before being overwhelmed by debt.

Poe was a habitual liar, always embroidering his past or trying to put a good face on bad circumstances. He never admitted, for example, that Sissy was ill with tuberculosis but always said that her poor health began with a "singing accident" when she had "broken a blood vessel" and started coughing blood.

Sissy spent six years as an invalid (sleeping on a straw bed, kept warm by Poe's old military coat and Catterina, the cat). Poe shuddered every time she coughed — his moods were dependent on her health each day — but refused to admit she was dying.

After she died at age twenty-four, he visited her grave at night, stealing from the house in his stocking feet so Muddy couldn't hear him and try to stop him.

But he also began courting four different women at the same time. Within two years he was engaged to a woman who lived directly across the street from the place where his mother was buried. Soon after that he was found unconscious on the street, his clothes in complete disarray.

He died four days later, at age forty, possibly from alcohol poisoning or inflammation of the brain. His last words were, "Lord, help my poor soul."

With him, it is said, was the miniature portrait of his mother.

ℬOOKMARKS

➥ As a boy, Poe liked to shock people by putting a sheet over his head and coming into the room as a ghost. His stories were full of shocking, creepy things as well. In "The Tell-Tale Heart," "The Pit and the Pendulum," "The Black Cat," "The Premature Burial," "The Imp of the Perverse," and other stories, Poe created ideas and techniques still used in modern horror stories and movies.

➥ "The Murders in the Rue Morgue" and Poe's other mysteries starring C. Auguste Dupin have provided the model for such amateur detectives as Sherlock Holmes (created by Sir Arthur Conan Doyle). At the time Poe was writing, the word *detective* did not yet exist in the English language. Today, the Edgar Awards, given each year by the Mystery Writers of America for the best mystery books, are named after him.

➥ "The Raven," Poe's best-known poem, had the effect a hit song might have today. It made Poe famous overnight and generated enormous praise and many imitations, especially of its refrain: "Quoth the raven 'Nevermore.'" "To hear Poe perform 'The Raven,'" wrote a fan, "which he does very quietly, is an event in one's life." Unfortunately, the poem earned Poe little money.

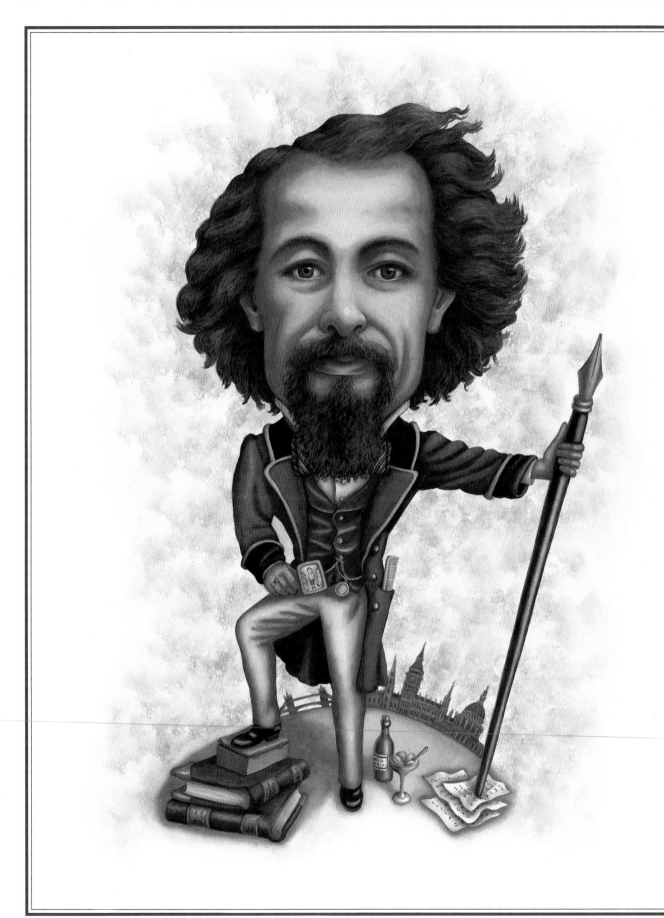

CHARLES DICKENS

BORN IN PORTSMOUTH, ENGLAND, 1812
DIED IN ROCHESTER, ENGLAND, 1870

*English novelist, especially known for the
great characters he created in* A Tale of Two Cities,
Great Expectations, *and many other books*

TWO DAYS AFTER his twelfth birthday, in a damp factory overrun with rats, Charles Dickens went to work to support his family. All day, with two meal breaks (often raisin pudding with a penny loaf of bread), he pasted labels on bottles of black shoe polish. Though his parents were very much alive (his father was in prison for debt — at the time, a crime), he never forgot his feeling of being orphaned.

Dickens eventually returned for two more years to school, where he wrote stories on scraps of paper and sold them to schoolmates for marbles. He later became a law clerk, a court reporter, a journalist — and with the publication of *The Pickwick Papers* when he was twenty-four, he was set for life.

As each new novel was published, Dickens became not only one of the most popular writers of all time but also the most popular public speaker of his day. He entertained people in an age without TV, radio, or movies, and his reading tours earned him pots of money. Audiences treated him as fans do rock stars now, mobbing him, ripping his clothes, lionizing him. His final home, a three-story house called Gad's Hill Place, was the very estate his father had often pointed out years

39

before as the place Dickens might live "if he would only work hard enough."

Dickens did work hard. When he wasn't on tour, he got up at seven o'clock, bathed in cold water, and wrote until lunch. He wrote neatly in blue ink with a goose-quill pen on blue-gray paper, completing two to four pages a day. If his writing wasn't going well, he doodled or picked fights with his wife, his ten children, or his servants. In the afternoon he tried to spend as many hours walking as he had writing—he would often walk twenty or thirty miles at a time, his dogs trotting behind him. He spent the evenings playing twenty questions and charades, and went to bed at midnight.

The objects on his desk had to be in exactly the same position each day before he could begin work, and his bed had to be set in a north-south direction before he could sleep. He touched certain objects three times for luck and thought of Friday as his lucky day. He was fascinated by ghosts, and he attended séances, murder trials, and public hangings whenever he could.

He was also fascinated by his own hair—if he thought a hair was out of place, he'd pull out a comb, even if he was at a dinner party. Notoriously vain, Dickens surrounded himself with mirrors. He wore flashy clothes: red velvet waistcoats, rings on his fingers, and a diamond stickpin on his vest.

For someone whose books were stuffed with descriptions of meals, Dickens drank and ate little — perhaps ham for breakfast and toasted cheese for dinner. In breaks during public readings, he would eat a dozen oysters and sip a little champagne.

His wife, in one of the most famous marriages of his century, was Catherine Hogarth. He called her Mouse and Dearest Pig, and later, when they were not getting along so well, Donkey. He grew impatient with her, and after sixteen years of marriage and amid much gossip from the neighbors, they separated. He kept custody of the children and became obsessed with an actress, Ellen Ternan.

All his life, Dickens was troubled by a pain in his side, an inflamed kidney that caused a fatal stroke at age fifty-eight. He was buried in Westminster Abbey, and thousands of people came for months afterward to pay their respects.

*B*OOKMARKS

 •◆ Although Dickens wrote *A Christmas Carol* (an immediate bestseller) mostly for money, the success of the novel helped to create something spiritual — the modern concept of the "Christmas spirit." Dickens was keenly aware of the security that money could bring, and it is said that Ebenezer Scrooge, the most famous miser in fiction, is partly based on himself.

 •◆ *Oliver Twist*, a novel about how poverty can breed crime, was the first book in the English language with a child as its hero; Oliver is still one of the most famous orphans in literature. No matter how rich Dickens became, he always had tremendous empathy for the children of his day, who often had hard lives.

 •◆ The death of Little Nell in *The Old Curiosity Shop* aroused unparalleled public response. Dickens's novels were published in installments, and crowds of Americans awaiting the next episode from overseas would gather at the New York harbor to ask English travelers tearfully, "Is Little Nell dead?"

 •◆ Dickens called *David Copperfield*, the novel that contains the most elements from his own life, his favorite of all his books.

CHARLOTTE AND EMILY BRONTË

BORN IN 1816 AND DIED IN 1855 IN YORKSHIRE, ENGLAND (CHARLOTTE)
BORN IN 1818 AND DIED IN 1848 IN YORKSHIRE, ENGLAND (EMILY)

English sisters famous for
Jane Eyre, Wuthering Heights,
and other novels and poetry

MANY CHILDREN MAKE UP imaginary kingdoms. But Charlotte and Emily Brontë were unique in the history of such inventions.

They created the world of Glass Town and peopled it with the "descendants" of their brother Branwell's twelve wooden soldiers. It had its own language (called the Young Men's Tongue), jokes, maps, heroes, constitution — and literature, which the children wrote in tiny print on scraps of paper they made into booklets. By the time Charlotte was fourteen, she had compiled twenty-two volumes, a total of 350 pages. Glass Town was her obsession even as an adult, as later the land of Gondal (where all the rulers were women) became Emily's.

The Brontë sisters spent almost their whole lives in a large stone house surrounded by steep moors covered with purple heather, where the wind always whistled. They had no neighbors. The warmth of summer never really arrived — the damp house always seemed bleak. It brooded over a graveyard, through which the water from the family's well was channeled.

By the time Charlotte was five and Emily was three, the graveyard included their mother's coffin. It is said that she died murmuring "Oh, my poor children" at the thought of leaving her six children in the care of their eccentric father, a clergyman. He kept a loaded pistol on him at all times and when angry would fire it out the back door. Because of his fear of fires, he refused to allow curtains, wallpaper, or carpets in the house. It was rumored that he gave the children nothing to eat except potatoes and that he destroyed any clothes he thought would encourage vanity. Her father, Charlotte said years later, "did not like children." He never ate meals with them and spent most of his time alone in his study. He did, however, tell them horrific ghost stories.

After the two oldest sisters died (as a result of appalling conditions at their boarding school), Charlotte, age nine, became a "little mother" to the family. People said that she looked like a little old woman within a few years. With her sense of duty and responsibility, she never put her own wishes first. Too near-sighted to play games with others, she was known as a "goody-goody," although she, like her father, told frightening ghost stories. She had a habit of wheeling around in her chair so that her face would be hidden from the person she was talking to. She was sure that she was so ugly that people would avert their eyes rather than look at her.

Convinced that she had to earn money to help send Branwell to school, Charlotte went to work at age nineteen as a teacher and governess, the only career then open to women. Intelligent but painfully shy, she was unhappy whenever she was away from the parsonage—though she admitted it was "buried away from the world." She thought of her students as "fat-headed oafs," and she constantly gritted her teeth at the "wretched bondage" of being, essentially, a family servant.

Emily was as brilliant as Charlotte, and even more strange. She had a mysterious smile and rarely talked. Restless and secretive, she would dart into a room to fetch a book without looking at anyone. An even bigger failure than Charlotte as a governess (Emily loathed the work), she paid as little attention to the real world as possible. Nicknamed the Major, she dominated Charlotte.

Emily seemed to like animals better than humans and took care of cats, geese, and her dogs—Tiger, Keeper, and Flossy. The dogs usually got part of her breakfast (oatmeal porridge). She could be headstrong and opinionated to the point of being unreasonable. She once cauterized her arm with a red-hot poker after she was bitten by a rabid dog, telling no one until it was healed. Another time she punished Keeper with a ferocious beating for sleeping on her clean white bedspread.

Emily was a head taller than Charlotte. Both were thin and wore plain, faded, homemade dresses and long, narrow shoes. Charlotte was so small that she wore children's underwear all her life. When they weren't writing, they taught Sunday school, took care of the sick in the village nearby, did needlework samplers, and cleaned house. They roamed the moors in all weather for hours at a time. At night the sisters read out loud but not usually their most private writings.

The parsonage was filled with books, newspapers, magazines—and lots of secrets. One day Charlotte discovered a notebook in the dining room and read the poetry that Emily and their sister, Anne, were secretly writing. Excited, Charlotte persuaded her sisters that the three of them should publish a book: *Poems by Currer, Ellis, and Acton Bell* (instead of Charlotte, Emily, and Anne Brontë). They used male names both to protect their privacy (from even their father and brother) and because they felt critics were prejudiced against women writers. The slim green book sold only two copies, but it inspired the sisters to continue with their other writing, which for Emily was the novel *Wuthering Heights.*

A year after it was published, Branwell died of alcohol poisoning and tuberculosis. Emily caught cold at his funeral and never completely recovered. Stubborn as ever, she did her chores even when she was too weak and disoriented to recognize her beloved heather. She refused all treatment until two hours before her death.

She died on the sofa in the dining room, at age thirty, of tuberculosis. Her coffin measured only sixteen inches across. Her dog Keeper lay outside her bedroom for a week afterward and howled.

Six months later Anne died, also of tuberculosis, and Charlotte was alone with her father, who still never ate meals with her. With the money from the publication of her novel *Jane Eyre,* she indulged herself a little — new dresses, a bonnet with pink lining, curtains for the house at last.

She continued to write, working neatly in pencil in little blank books, on a table in the dining room. When she was asked how she wrote about things she had never experienced — taking opium, for example — she said that she would think about a situation or a subject so many nights before falling asleep that it would seem as if she really had experienced it and could describe it. The first time she saw the ocean, she burst into tears and couldn't speak for the rest of the day. She was always honest, offering even unpopular opinions, and was known to cast a chill over whole dinner parties with her pronouncements. Still, she had friends and admirers, and when she stayed with the rich and famous, she was always especially kind to their governesses.

Several men proposed to her, but she never felt excited enough to "want to die" for them, so she never accepted. Her father's assistant, Arthur Bell Nicholls, was so persistent that she finally agreed to marry him, partly out of pity. Her new husband didn't approve of "Currer Bell." All her life, Charlotte had been told that literary ambition was unsuitable in a woman, and after her marriage she stopped writing.

Within nine months she was dead, at age thirty-eight, possibly from tuberculosis complicated by pregnancy. She was buried in the graveyard outside the parsonage with the rest of her family, except for her father.

The man who had seen all six of his children die young lived on alone, dying at age eighty-three.

*B*OOKMARKS

◆ Charlotte began writing *Jane Eyre* just after nursing her father through a painful eye operation, in pain herself with a severe toothache (she eventually lost all her teeth), depressed from constant rejection of a previous novel, and with a bleak view of the future. The new novel was successful but also controversial. Her strong governess-heroine (Jane) and unconventional hero (Rochester) made the author notorious, someone "to keep one's daughters away from." *Jane Eyre* was "a wicked book" and "truly offensive." Charlotte herself was unmoved. "I am ashamed of nothing I have written — not a line," she maintained near the end of her life.

◆ Emily modeled Heathcliff, the romantic, haunted central character in *Wuthering Heights*, partly on her troubled brother Branwell, and the location of the novel was based partly on the stormy weather (described as "wuthering") around her own home. When the sisters read chapters to each other by firelight, Charlotte complained that scenes from *Wuthering Heights* were keeping her awake at night. Reviewers were more outspoken. They called the novel demonic, sickening, and the most shocking book ever published. Today it is often considered a better book than *Jane Eyre*, but when it was published, reviewers compared it unfavorably to Charlotte's book. In a modern movie version of *Wuthering Heights*, rock musician Sinéad O'Connor plays the part of Emily writing her book.

EMILY DICKINSON

BORN IN 1830 AND DIED IN 1886
IN AMHERST, MASSACHUSETTS

Considered one of the greatest American poets,
famous for 1,775 poems published
mostly after her death

THE MOST MYSTERIOUS and eccentric of all writers may be Emily Dickinson. Shy and awkward as a teen, she was nevertheless popular at fudge parties, picnics in the hills, sleigh rides, and — at the first sign of spring — maple sugar parties. Her favorite game all her life was hide-and-seek.

Her role, as the daughter of a well-to-do lawyer, was to stay home and help with housework until the time came to marry.

But the time never came. Instead, she described the dictionary as her "only companion" and books as "the strongest friend." She ran upstairs if the doorbell rang. As she did her chores — baking cookies, frying doughnuts, working in her garden — she jotted poetry in the margin of the newspaper or on scraps of brown grocery paper. In her corner room, warmed by its own stove, she would make a clean copy of a poem in ink, thread it together with a few other poems, and place the booklet in a locked box in her cherrywood bureau. She loved to be alone in her room, free from interruption, or out for long walks with her shaggy brown dog, Carlo.

She chose to write and think "in [her] own Society" rather than the society outside, with its restrictions on women. She left Amherst no more than a dozen times, mainly to go to Boston to have her constant eye trouble treated.

Dickinson went out of her way to avoid meeting people, but she had no fear of writing letters to famous, important men of the day. The first time one correspondent met her, she slipped two orange day lilies into his hand; "I never see strangers and hardly know what to say," she said under her breath.

Her stern, powerful father rarely noticed her and instead favored his son (whose letters he compared to Shakespeare's work, while he never read a poem written by Emily). Yet after her father's death, she withdrew completely and seldom left her house again before her own death eleven years later. The house was quiet inside, with heavy furniture and drawn curtains, the air thick with the smell of flowers.

After Dickinson once lowered a basket containing fresh gingerbread to some children playing on the lawn below her room, children in the neighborhood took

to peeking through the tall hemlock hedges, hoping for a glimpse of her. They seldom succeeded. She wouldn't even see the dressmaker who made her white dresses (over the years she stopped wearing clothes with color in them). Her sister Lavinia went to fittings for her. Nor would she expose her handwriting; when she wrote letters, she had "Vinnie" address the envelopes.

When Dickinson became ill, she allowed the doctor to examine her only from the next room; he would watch her walk past the doorway. She was fifty-five when she died of a kidney ailment, though it was said she looked much younger. Dressed in white and holding two heliotropes, she was buried next to her parents in a white casket covered with violets. Poems by Emily Brontë were read at her funeral.

Her sister lived on alone — except for the company of thirty cats — in the Dickinson house. When Vinnie found the box full of Emily's poems, she became obsessed with getting them published. From that point on, Emily Dickinson's place in literature was established.

$\mathscr{B}$OOKMARKS

➴ Dickinson's poems are known by their first lines, as in "After great pain, a formal feeling comes," "Because I could not stop for Death," "I'll tell you how the Sun rose," and "I'm Nobody! Who are you?" Only a few of them were published, anonymously and possibly against her will, while she was alive. She called her poems snow to indicate their purity from the world of money. It was a point of honor with her not to publish: "How can you print a piece of your own soul?"

➴ Dickinson defined poetry this way: "If I feel physically as if the top of my head were taken off, I know *that* is poetry." Her first publishers may have feared the same feeling: they made many changes to the poems to avoid offending readers with Dickinson's innovative rhythms and unconventional way of expressing herself. While her poetry was considered too strange and serious at first, today many modern poets think of her as their "patron saint."

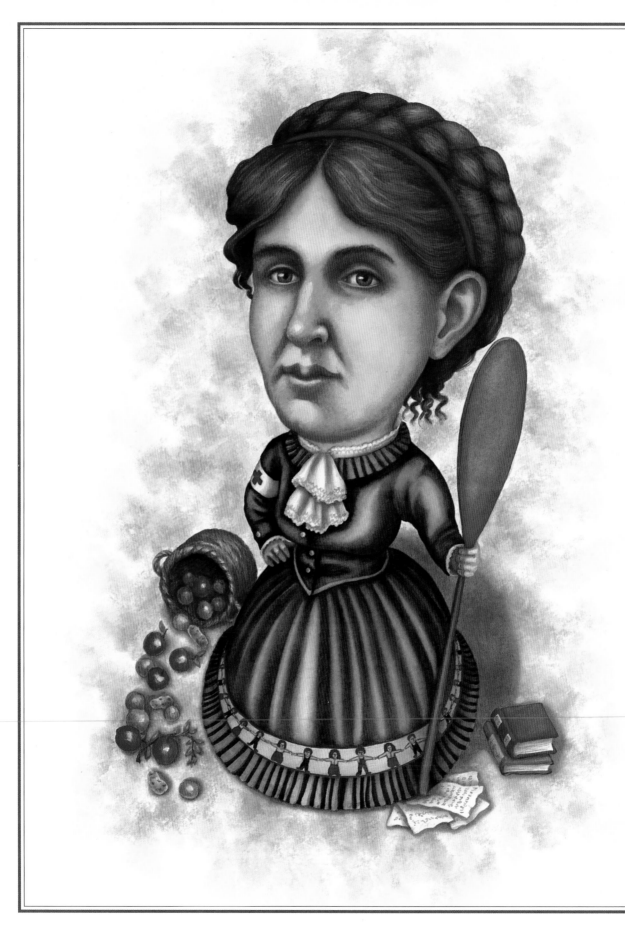

LOUISA MAY ALCOTT

BORN IN GERMANTOWN, PENNSYLVANIA, 1832
DIED IN CONCORD, MASSACHUSETTS, 1888

American novelist famous for Little Women *and other novels for children, as well as short stories she called lurid*

BRONSON ALCOTT, a well-known philosopher and educator, did not believe in working for wages. The result? A family "as poor as rats," according to Louisa May, one of his four daughters.

The Alcotts moved around. For a time they lived at Fruitlands, a communal farm that did not allow cotton (because it was a product of slavery), silk (because it exploited silkworms), or wool (because it belonged to sheep).

When the family had money they ate vegetables. Otherwise a meal might consist of apples and bread. If Louisa was bad, she got no dinner at all. Her father found her willful and called her demonic. She was always taking dares, like rubbing red peppers into her eyes or jumping off the barn (and spraining both ankles). She felt "more boy than girl" and spent hours fantasizing a better life: "I'll be rich and famous and happy before I die, see if I won't."

Alcott came to believe she was the only one who could save her "pathetic" family. She started selling stories at sixteen and was soon the sole breadwinner.

53

She worked as an army nurse during the Civil War until she fell ill with typhoid pneumonia. The "cure" gave her mercury poisoning, so she was never fully healthy again, but the whole experience led to her first successful book, *Hospital Sketches*, a collection of her letters home.

Alcott locked herself in her room to write as many as fourteen hours a day. She worked neatly, pressing so hard with a steel pen that her right thumb became permanently paralyzed. She took breaks to run in the nearby woods. Her mother (who called her Louy or Lu) would bring in cups of tea and gingerbread slices, or a squash pie for dinner, while her father (who called her Weedy) offered cups of cider or a red apple.

The publication of *Little Women* brought instant fame and wiped out every debt the Alcotts had ever had.

Alcott continued to push herself. Subsequent books installed a furnace and carpets in the family house, bought schooling and trips to Europe for her artist sister, and ensured security for various relatives.

But fame annoyed Alcott. Her appearance was so no-nonsense that neighborhood children sometimes cried upon meeting her. She looked older than her age, sad, and suspicious, and had thick chestnut hair piled on her head. Though her work describes current clothing styles in loving detail, she dressed plainly (in black or dark brown) and conveyed the impression that she despised fashion.

When necessary she did chores, such as baking bread or making applesauce and cocoa. She liked to try experimental potions, and she was a health-conscious vegetarian.

Alcott never married. She had crushes on the writers Ralph Waldo Emerson (she left wildflowers on his doorstep) and Henry David Thoreau, who were both friends of her father. But when her heroes were unattainable, she didn't seem to mind: "I would rather be a free spinster and paddle my own canoe." She was an ardent supporter of the right of women to vote.

Bronson Alcott died at age eighty-eight. Louisa died two days later, her body having grown steadily weaker from the mercury poisoning. She was fifty-five.

At their joint funeral, the minister said, "So this daughter, such a support to her father on earth, was needed by him even in heaven."

ℬOOKMARKS

➥ *Little Women,* the story of four sisters growing up in a New England town, is the first part of a trilogy (followed by *Little Men* and *Jo's Boys*) based on Alcott and her family. Alcott modeled tomboyish, literary Jo March after herself: "I am Jo," she told people. She wrote *Little Women* merely to fulfill the many requests for a "girls'" book; the work was not enjoyable to her. She thought the novel was "boring" and wished that some of its success would rub off on her favorite work, *Moods,* a serious book for adults.

➥ Alcott had a secret life. Under the name A. M. Barnard, she wrote short stories she called lurid (which to her meant lively and forbidden). Tales such as "Pauline's Passion and Punishment" and "The Skeleton in the Closet" involved powerful women, murder, suicide, madness, passion, and drug experimentation. Such "rubbishy tales" paid the best, Alcott discovered — they "keep the family cozy."

Mark Twain

BORN IN FLORIDA, MISSOURI, 1835
DIED NEAR REDDING, CONNECTICUT, 1910

Considered the greatest American humorist, creator of
Tom Sawyer, Huckleberry Finn, The Prince and the Pauper,
and other influential works

"SAMUEL LANGHORNE CLEMENS!" yelled the teacher, her patience gone.

The boy whose name she called knew that when a teacher uses your whole name it means trouble. And he always was in some kind of trouble — for putting snakes in his aunt's sewing basket, hiding bats in his pockets for his mother to find, or perhaps faking death to get out of going to school. Once, from a height of three stories, he dropped a watermelon shell onto his brother's head. "I was born excited," he admitted.

Later, perhaps wanting to turn over a new leaf, he took a new name. Growing up on the Mississippi River in Hannibal, Missouri, he was fascinated by the steamboats that brought tourists and entertainers. His boyhood dream, which he fulfilled at age twenty-three, was to become a licensed riverboat pilot. *Mark twain* is a Mississippi River expression that means "safe water — twelve feet deep," and by age twenty-eight, he was using this phrase as his pen name.

Twain first went to work at age eleven when his father died, always taking a book along for companionship. He worked in print shops and newspaper offices,

prospected for gold and silver out West, and traveled to Hawaii and came back to lecture about it.

His first appearance in a magazine was as Mike Swain (the editor couldn't read Twain's handwriting), author of "Forty-Three Days in an Open Boat." A thrilling account of the survivors of a disaster at sea, this was a big story Twain almost didn't get to write. Much to his embarrassment, on the day he was to interview the survivors, he was suffering so badly from saddle sores that he had to be carried to the meeting on a stretcher and take his notes lying down.

The first time he ever told a funny story, he discovered that he loved, above all else, being "killingly" funny. His sense of humor became his trademark. With his humorous short story "The Celebrated Jumping Frog of Calaveras County," Mark Twain fell into writing and stayed.

On their first date, Twain took Olivia Langdon, whom he later married, to hear Charles Dickens speak. Olivia called her husband Youth or Little Man. All during their marriage, she acted as his first reader, using a pencil to cross out any part of his writing she didn't like. They had four children.

The best compliment Twain ever got was when his daughter Susy praised the "perfectly delightful" stories he would tell her and her sister, Clara, as they perched on the arms of his chair. He had total recall of his own childhood, things both happy and sad — "A boy's life is not all comedy" — and used the material throughout his books.

Wealthy from his writing, Twain amazed the neighbors by building the most elaborate and eccentric house in Hartford, Connecticut — it had nineteen luxurious rooms, plus five bathrooms. (The neighbors included Harriet Beecher Stowe, famous as the author of *Uncle Tom's Cabin.*) He slept in a black bed with carved angels on it that was large enough to hold a whole family. He spent summers at Quarry Farm, near Elmira, New York, where he wrote in a small, eight-sided room lined with windows. He had the travel bug and would live in Europe for years at a time.

As much money as Twain made, he would often lose it by investing in the wrong gadgets. Once he lost $200,000 on a failed typesetting machine. When he was offered a chance to invest in Alexander Graham Bell's new telephone, he turned it down as too risky. (Later, however, he owned the first telephone ever installed in a private house . . . where he got calls day and night.)

Whenever he went bankrupt, he would do another lecture tour to make his money back. Twain's tours were world famous. He enjoyed performing. He simply liked to hear himself talk, and indeed, he wasn't happy unless he was dominating a conversation. Luckily, people hung on his every word. Hardly a day passed without a reporter seeking his opinion on something, and he was thought to be the most photographed man in the world — so famous that there was even a Mark Twain impersonator working in Australia. He felt like the "most conspicuous person on the planet" — but on most days he liked the attention.

Twain took a day off now and then to go skating or play with his children, but most often he worked, frequently in bed. When rheumatism affected his writing arm, he became the first professional writer to use a typewriter. Protective of his good reputation, he would burn whole manuscripts if he felt they weren't up to his usual standards.

Twain's favorite escape was to play pool. Sometimes he stayed up and played all night. He also liked to watch baseball, and he loved to read his writings aloud to his family. For exercise he took ten-mile walks in the country. He carried cats around on his shoulders and gave them names like Lazy, Satan, Sin, Cleveland, Pestilence, and Famine.

Twain was not known as a fighter. He had left the Civil War after just two weeks, weary (as he joked) from "persistent retreating." He would leave town rather than fight a duel. He even avoided touching other people — he was not a backslapper. But he did have a temper. Once, when a button was missing from the third shirt he tried on in a row (he designed his own shirts; they buttoned in back), he threw all the shirts out the window and screamed swear words loud enough to wake up the neighborhood.

Twain wore white clothes, winter and summer. He said they made him feel "clean in a dirty world." He ordered his trademark white linen suits from his tailor six at a time. Around the house he lounged about in slippers, and he wore a long nightgown to bed. He kept his bushy hair shiny by washing it every day and rubbing the shampoo lather off with a coarse towel. He smoked as many as forty cigars a day; his idea of moderation was "never smoke more than one cigar at a time."

As funny as he was, Twain always looked serious and older than his age. When he was sad, he played hymns on the piano.

Three of Twain's children died before he did, as did his beloved wife. Shortly after his youngest daughter died, when Twain was seventy-four, he found her Christmas present to him: a large globe, something he had always wanted. Overcome by sadness, he stopped writing, and four months later, he slipped into a coma and died of heart disease. His last words were about Robert Louis Stevenson's *The Strange Case of Dr. Jekyll and Mr. Hyde.*

Twain might not have liked this book. He thought that a person's real life story is lived inside that person's head: "And *that* you can never know."

ℬOOKMARKS

•❖ The most famous fence in American literature is the one Tom Sawyer tricked his friends into painting for him. Twain created this scene while he was living in London. He wrote much of *Tom Sawyer* quickly, completing as many as fifty pages a day — but as with almost all his books, he ran out of steam in the middle and set the story aside for two years before completing it. Most of the adventures in *Tom Sawyer* really happened, according to Twain. The book sold two million copies while he was alive and continues to be his most popular work.

•❖ American writer Ernest Hemingway once said that "all modern American literature comes from . . . *Huckleberry Finn."* Many consider this sequel to *Tom Sawyer* to be America's greatest novel — but it is also controversial. Banned upon publication as "trash" because of its nonstandard grammar and Huck's "casual morals," it is sometimes banned now because of Huck's acceptance of racial stereotypes. Twain did not think of himself as a racist; he thought *Huck Finn* was about equality and the universal dreams of all people. He hated slavery, was ashamed of the way whites treated blacks, and paid the expenses of the first black students at Yale Law School and various colleges.

FRANCES HODGSON BURNETT

BORN IN MANCHESTER, ENGLAND, 1849
DIED ON LONG ISLAND, NEW YORK, 1924

English-American creator of The Secret Garden,
Sara Crewe (A Little Princess), *and*
Little Lord Fauntleroy

WHEN A STRICT teacher once cut her arm with a riding whip, Frances Hodgson Burnett stared at the cut for a moment. Then she looked up at the teacher and laughed in his face.

All her life, Burnett was tough. Yet at the same time, she tried to heed her mother's constant warning: "Remember to always be a little lady."

Burnett's mother was left with five children, all under age eight, when her prosperous husband died. The family drifted from England to live with Burnett's uncle in rural Tennessee. Burnett spent afternoons reading in a place she called the Bower, which had a roof of grapevines and a floor of pine needles.

As a teen, Burnett felt responsible for supporting the family. To earn money for paper and the postage to mail her first stories, she picked wild grapes. Calling herself a "pen-driving machine, warranted not to wear out," she soon boasted that she could write a story about anything, even a fly on the ceiling if she had to. Reading her own books made her laugh and cry.

Her books also made her the wealthiest writer in Britain or America. Burnett was admired by royalty, politicians, and many writers of the day (Mark Twain wanted to collaborate on a book with her). She lived well — "money is made for spending" — and loved to play "fairy godmother." She enjoyed furnishing the various houses she lived in. One had twenty-two rooms, each dominated by a single color; her bedroom was pink. She also liked to furnish dollhouses; the last one she owned had a working shower. Above all, she liked to bring about "happy endings" for family, friends, neighbors, strangers, and various charities.

Many people adored her, but others thought her conceited. Some said she could find a compliment about herself in a weather report. She was always plump, and her nickname was Fluffy. She wore flowing chiffon dresses with miles of lace, cloaks lined with white satin and ermine, and black velvet hats with what she described as "insane" feathers.

Burnett married twice. Both husbands were doctors who also acted as her business managers; the second was ten years younger than she was. But she was living apart from her husband soon after each marriage. Burnett didn't like being married—she thought it got in the way of her work.

"The one perfect thing in my life was the childhood of my boys," she once said. Her two sons called her Dearest and brought her small treasures (twigs, pebbles, newspaper pictures); she would curl their hair while they sat in front of the fire.

Burnett was ahead of her time. After one of her divorces, a newspaper reporter wrote, "She entertained very advanced ideas as to the rights of women and the duties of a wife." She was the first woman smoker many people saw (alternating puffs on Turkish cigarettes with bites of peppermint creams). Believing that films were the wave of the future, she let several of her books be made into movies.

The opening of the film *Little Lord Fauntleroy,* starring Mary Pickford, was Burnett's last appearance in public. She died of heart disease at age seventy-four, looking out her window at her beds of chrysanthemums and dahlias.

*B*OOKMARKS

➥ *The Secret Garden,* the story of "disagreeable" Mary Lennox, has been called the most satisfying children's book ever. The story has been retold in a popular Broadway musical, touring productions, and five movie adaptations. Burnett got the idea for *The Secret Garden* in the rose garden at her house in England, planted with three hundred rose bushes from France. She finished the book at her villa on Long Island, surrounded by rows of candytuft, nasturtium, and phlox. "When you have a garden, you have a future," she once wrote.

➥ Burnett's son Vivian was the model for *Little Lord Fauntleroy,* a Cinderella story for boys. The tale inspired toys, chocolates, perfume, four movie versions, a Broadway play that ran for four years—and a notorious fashion trend: dressing boys in long curls and black velvet suits with lace cuffs and collars. Later, when male reporters and reviewers were increasingly unkind to Burnett and her work, it was said that boys who had been so dressed were now grown up and seeking revenge.

ROBERT LOUIS STEVENSON

BORN IN EDINBURGH, SCOTLAND, 1850
DIED IN SAMOA, 1894

Scottish novelist and poet, famous for
Treasure Island, Kidnapped, A Child's Garden of Verses, *and*
The Strange Case of Dr. Jekyll and Mr. Hyde

ROBERT LOUIS STEVENSON spent his whole life either ill in bed or out having thrilling adventures.

He had tuberculosis and was frequently thought to be dying. He did most of his writing in bed, wearing a red flannel dressing gown, propped among pillows with a pencil in his hand and a pad of paper on his knees. Writing was an escape: "It's such fun just to give way and let your pen go off with you into the uttermost parts of the earth and the mountains of the moon."

When Stevenson was a young man he dressed shabbily, in black flannel shirts and a hat so worn out that some people couldn't tell what it was. He liked to live on the wild side and he didn't like the rules of society. He believed, for example, that conventional marriage was hypocritical because it subordinated women.

He met Fanny Osbourne, a married American art student eleven years his senior, when he jumped in through the window of her hotel. After her divorce, she became his wife, nurse, and literary sounding board. She thought he was beautiful.

He agreed, and never passed a mirror without checking out his reflection.

Some people thought he was a little affected, but his friends, who called him Louis, described him as "lovable," "entrancing," and "the most fascinating human being I have ever known." He was thought of as a man who never grew up. Despite his illness, he had a positive attitude and never lost his "goblin laughter."

The Stevensons, along with Fanny's two children from her first marriage, traveled continuously in search of a climate that would keep Stevenson well. Voyaging on a yacht on the South Seas proved exhilarating, and they finally settled on the island of Samoa, where they built a large house they called Vailima ("Five Rivers"). When times were good, they had huge feasts with their Samoan neighbors. When times were hard, the family might have to make a meal out of one avocado. The Samoans called Stevenson Tusitala ("Teller of Tales") and built a road to his house that they called the Road of the Loving Heart.

Stevenson wrote alone in his room all day, then came out to prepare dinner with Fanny. He sometimes read aloud to her what he had written. He smoked continuously, and he could talk about wine so extravagantly that listeners found themselves too distracted to even taste it.

Stevenson was thin, a "bag of bones," and energetic. He loved to talk, prowling the room like a panther; the greatest punishment for him was when doctors ordered him to stay quiet in bed. The most he could do then was play with toy soldiers or take lumps of wax and mold tiny figures and landscapes.

Stevenson died at age forty-four of a stroke, not the tuberculosis that had plagued him much of his life. He was making the salad dressing for dinner and put his hand to his head. "Do I look strange?" he asked Fanny. He died within hours. The Samoan chiefs buried him on the mountain behind Vailima.

His gravestone is inscribed with his own poem "Requiem": "Here he lies where he longed to be; / Home is the sailor, home from the sea."

*B*OOKMARKS

•• One day when Stevenson's stepson Lloyd was bored and sick, Stevenson tried to distract him with a paint box. They painted a map, which inspired a story about Long John Silver and buried treasure. Stevenson began writing it down, to make a "book for boys," and *Treasure Island* turned out to be the book that put Stevenson on the literary map.

•• People usually think of *A Child's Garden of Verses* as a collection of lighthearted poems about childhood, but many of the poems are actually about painful days and endless nights in bed. Stevenson even wrote the book in bed, in partial darkness, when he was in his thirties. He worked with his left hand when his right was tied to his side by the doctor treating his most recent lung hemorrhage.

•• When Fanny woke Stevenson from a bad nightmare one night, he wasn't pleased, for she had interrupted a "fine bogey tale." The next morning he began to turn the dream into a book. When it was finished, he read it aloud to Fanny, who criticized it for being too much like the work of Edgar Allan Poe. Angry, Stevenson tossed it into the fire and started over. The final result was *The Strange Case of Dr. Jekyll and Mr. Hyde,* one of the most famous horror stories ever written.

JACK LONDON

BORN IN SAN FRANCISCO, CALIFORNIA, 1876
DIED NEAR GLEN ELLEN, CALIFORNIA, 1916

*American writer known for novels and short stories
about survival, including* The Call of the Wild,
White Fang, *and "To Build a Fire"*

JACK LONDON PACKED many lifetimes into his forty years.

He grew up poor after his father, an astrologer, deserted the family before London was born. At age thirteen he worked in a cannery fourteen hours a day and then (as his mother said) "fell in with bad company." By day he was known as Prince of the Oyster Pirates for his skill in raiding the oyster beds of San Francisco Bay; nights were spent at the First and Last Chance Saloon. He traveled about on freight trains and ships, and by age eighteen was in jail for vagrancy.

Tired of being a "work beast" and wanting to live by his wits, he began writing fifteen hours a day, forgetting to eat, working on an old typewriter that gave him bleeding blisters and kept his neighbors awake. Rejection slips piled five feet high.

Then he joined the gold rush north to the Klondike. Living on bread, beans, and bacon grease, London did not strike gold . . . until *writing* about the Klondike made him, at age twenty-nine, the most highly paid and widely read author in America.

London reminded many people of a Greek god, with his handsome, tanned face, strong neck, and eyes that appeared to change color. He lost most of his teeth, often in fights, but he was enormously proud of his body. His image as a ladies' man and rowdy brawler became so exaggerated that other men, when they got into trouble, would pretend to be him.

London left his first wife, Bess Maddern, and their two daughters to marry Charmian Kittredge, who was five years older than he was. They called each other Mate-Woman and Mate-Man. She typed and edited his books and participated in all his adventures.

He loved to box (especially with Charmian), fly kites, and ride bikes and horses. In Hawaii he was one of the first Americans to learn how to surf. He worked as a war correspondent all over the world, and he ran for mayor of Oakland several times, though he never was elected. (Sometimes his books were banned because of his controversial politics.) In his biggest adventure of all, he built a boat he called the *Snark* and sailed it around the world for several years.

London did everything in a big way. When he bought his ranch in California, he planted sixty thousand eucalyptus trees and threw himself into raising stallions and growing grapes. London believed that, through willpower, anyone can do anything. Sometimes he was stubborn and arrogant, and he never took the blame for anything that went wrong.

He had a personal valet, who every evening arranged London's pencils and papers on his desk. London worked at night, sleeping on and off for five hours. In the afternoons he joined guests at the ranch for sports, practical jokes, and challenges — a guest might have to swallow a live goldfish or push peanuts up his nose. After dinner (London liked to eat raw meat — a "cannibal sandwich" of raw beef, perhaps, and as many as two barely cooked wild ducks a day), he played cards or read aloud until it was time to go back to his room to work. He was never seen without a cigarette and was a very heavy drinker.

London died at age forty from an overdose of the pain-killing drugs he took for a kidney obstruction. Whether the overdose was accidental or suicidal is a matter of controversy. His last words to Charmian were, "Thank God, you're not afraid of anything!"

His ashes were buried on the ranch, under a red boulder.

Bookmarks

●◆ *The Call of the Wild,* the classic dog story, describes how a tame dog named Buck reverts to the wild behavior of a wolf in order to survive. London based Buck on a dog named Jack, who was a cross between a St. Bernard and a Scots shepherd, that he had known in the Yukon.

●◆ *White Fang* tells the opposite story, of a wolf-dog that is gradually domesticated. London jokingly called it *The Call of the Tamed.* Wolves were important to London. One of his nicknames was Wolf; he owned a husky named Brown Wolf; the house he built on his Beauty Ranch in the Valley of the Moon was called Wolf House. (Two weeks before the last touches on its lavish twenty-two rooms were finished, the house burned down under mysterious circumstances.)

CARL SANDBURG

BORN IN GALESBURG, ILLINOIS, 1878
DIED NEAR FLAT ROCK, NORTH CAROLINA, 1967

American poet most famous for Chicago Poems,
Good Morning, America, *and his collection of humorous
American fairy tales*, Rootabaga Stories

CARL SANDBURG was born on a corn-husk mattress in a tiny cottage near the railroad tracks; his diapers were made from flour sacks. He kept everyone guessing as to how he would turn out. He was in jail at fourteen for swimming in the nude in a city pond, and later for riding a freight train without paying the fare. He lived for years as a hobo, often going without food in order to afford books. He worked as a fire fighter, a traveling salesman, and the secretary to the mayor of Milwaukee.

Then, after corresponding by mail but seeing her only a few times, he married a teacher and translator named Lilian Steichen (sister of the famous photographer Edward Steichen), whom he called Paula. She worked as his full-time secretary and, in her spare time, raised prize-winning goats. Sandburg said she was "the kind of woman I would be if I were a woman." Her encouragement made him decide to focus on poetry. On their fifty-fifth anniversary, Sandburg said that if it weren't for Paula he would have been a bum.

Sandburg held various newspaper jobs and wrote poetry late into the night. For seven years he worked as a movie critic, watching up to six movies a week (he loved

Charlie Chaplin). He and his wife were married for twenty years before they took their first vacation alone together (to Florida).

A friend described Sandburg as one of the most "successfully alive human beings I ever saw." He had a bronzed, rugged face that seemed chiseled out of stone and long hair (rival poet Robert Frost criticized his haircut). He ate simple food: home-made cheese and butter on pumpernickel bread and goat's milk. He liked to "horizontalize" (take a nap) after a meal, and he smoked cigars.

At age twelve he had experienced disaster while speaking in public (he forgot the speech), but as an adult he practiced lectures to rows of corn and cabbage heads, and eventually loved to perform. Sandburg collected folk songs on his travels and, breaking into song with his rich deep voice, was always the life of the party. His favorite song was "Hallelujah, I'm a Bum."

Sandburg's last home was Connemara, a secluded twenty-two-room mansion and farm surrounded by the Blue Ridge Mountains. Every room was lined with books, some fourteen thousand in all. His workroom on the third floor had many windows and a wood stove, with papers in fruit crates and poetry in wire baskets. On his desk were pine cones and ginkgo leaves collected on his walks — sometimes twenty miles a day, perhaps pulling one of his three daughters in a wagon behind him. To relax he played golf, and his favorite dog was named Bosco. He owned a tan sedan but was too easily distracted to drive.

He knew U.S. presidents and actress Marilyn Monroe (she sent him her poems), appeared on all the TV talk shows from "Today" to "Tonight," and won many prizes, including two Pulitzers. (The only award he looked at every day was from the National Association for the Advancement of Colored People. It named him a lifetime member of NAACP for his support of civil rights.) His favorite honor was to have a school named after him — there are at least twenty-four.

Sandburg died at age eighty-nine of heart and lung trouble. His wife filled his room with magnolia blossoms and played Chopin as he lay dying. His last word was her name. His ashes lie under a granite boulder in Galesburg, Illinois, his birthplace.

*B*OOKMARKS

➡ Sandburg wrote "Chicago," one of his most famous poems, during what he called the Dark Period, when he couldn't find a steady job and his family was at its poorest. The magazine that finally published the poem received many complaints — Sandburg's style was always controversial, and some people didn't even think that what he wrote should be called poetry (they called him a sledgehammer writer). When "Chicago" won a prize as the best American poem of the year, Sandburg observed that the two hundred-dollar prize money would "just octuple our bank account."

➡ "Fog," his most frequently quoted poem, was written when Sandburg was on his way to interview a judge for a newspaper. As he passed through Grant Park, he noticed the fog coming into the Chicago harbor. When the judge kept him waiting, he took out a pencil and wrote the poem in his vest-pocket notebook.

➡ Sandburg tried out the *Rootabaga Stories*, his original fairy tales, on "the homey-glomeys" (his daughters) first, asking them for advice at the dinner table. He introduced the stories to adults while he was eating German pancakes and wiener schnitzel with friends at a popular Chicago restaurant. The Potato Face Blind Man, a central character, is based on Sandburg himself. (Sandburg often worried that he would go blind and wore a green eyeshade when he was working.)

E. B. White

BORN IN MOUNT VERNON, NEW YORK, 1899
DIED IN NORTH BROOKLIN, MAINE, 1985

*American writer known for essays and
children's books:* Charlotte's Web, Stuart Little,
and The Trumpet of the Swan

"HELLO, EILEEN? This is Elwyn White." He had practiced this greeting so many times that when the mother of the girl he wanted to date answered the phone instead of the girl herself, he was unable to change the words. How embarrassing! Eileen still went out with him, for as nervous and uncomfortable as Elwyn Brooks White could be, he was charming, too.

The youngest of six children, White (always called Andy after college) had a happy, secure childhood. He grew up to be a private person who lived just the way he wanted to, once he figured out what that was. As a young man he sold roach powder, played the piano, tried being a reporter (though writing about murders made him ill), and drove a Model T Ford (named Hotspur, for a character from a Shakespeare play) across the country.

When he was twenty-six, he bought the first issue of a new magazine called *The New Yorker,* and for the rest of his life he wrote for it. He even married it, in a way, when he wed Katharine Angell, who was seven years older than he was and his boss. His idea of a compliment was to tell her, "You smell like pencil shavings."

The Whites, with Katharine's two children from an earlier marriage and their own son, Joel, moved to a remote farm in Maine. A woodshed connected the barn and the twelve-room house; White thought the place looked like a writer's house. He and Katharine had large offices. His looked out toward the road and mailbox and had a grand piano.

He liked to be the first person up in the mornings, lighting the fires, reading "Dear Abby," making coffee. White loved farm chores so much (and there was a never-ending supply of them) that he tended to write only on rainy days. To concentrate, he often wrote in the boathouse at the nearby lake. To relax, he hopped on his three-speed bike and took off. Evenings were for reading aloud, and Thursday nights were set aside for reading *Time* magazine.

White's favorite book was Henry David Thoreau's *Walden.* He took it everywhere and gave copies away as gifts. The book he thought was most important to the survival of the world was Rachel Carson's *Silent Spring;* he was concerned about pollution of all types. White was also an advocate of world peace — he thought all countries should have the same flag. Some newspapers called White's beliefs dangerous.

"Keep it simple!" was White's favorite expression. He didn't want to own too many possessions, except for his car (a Mercedes) and his boats (he preferred sailing to writing). He always had dogs; his last two were named Jones and Susy.

White had a terrible fear of public speaking, and he didn't try to conquer it. He won many awards but always found an excuse for not attending the ceremonies. He was sometimes so withdrawn that he seemed forbidding — unless he was showing off his latest goslings, ducklings, or chicks. As he grew older, he hardly ever left the farm except for doctor appointments.

White complained of so many ailments that his friends teased him about hypochondria. He was known to wear a surgical mask in public to protect him from contagious diseases. His appetite was notoriously small (except when it came to imported caviar); he felt sick when he would eat, and again when he didn't.

When Katharine died, White mourned that he had "lost the one thing that seemed to make any sense in my life." He lived for eight more years, still bike-riding and canoeing. He died at age eighty-six.

There were crowds of people at his memorial service, but White himself would have dreaded the thought of attending such a ceremony in his honor.

𝓑OOKMARKS

➻ White was one person who wasn't afraid of spiders. Once he let hundreds of them hatch and build webs atop his dresser. Pigs also fascinated him, so much that he began wondering why he took such good care of a pig when he was only going to kill and eat it. These interests inspired the creation of the most famous spider and pig in literature; White wrote *Charlotte's Web* in his boathouse. An instant best-seller, it is still the top-selling children's paperback novel today.

➻ After the idea for *Stuart Little* came to White in a dream, he began telling stories about his "dream mouse" to Joel and his nieces and nephews. It took him a long time to get around to writing the stories down; he finally did so during a period when he was most worried about his health.

➻ White's graceful essays influenced a whole generation of writers, as did his revision of William Strunk's writing manual, *The Elements of Style,* now known to writers everywhere as Strunk and White. In 1978 White was awarded a special Pulitzer Prize for "many years and many kinds of writing."

ZORA NEALE HURSTON

BORN IN EATONVILLE, FLORIDA, 1901?
DIED IN FORT PIERCE, FLORIDA, 1960

*American writer famous for novels and
collections of folklore that reveal aspects of
African-American culture*

ZORA NEALE HURSTON grew up strong and proud in an all-black town founded and run by African-Americans. Her father, a three-term mayor of Eatonville, thought Zora had too much spirit. But her mother urged her to "jump at the sun"—not necessarily to land there but at least to get off the ground.

Hurston first landed in New York, where she perfected her "Eatonville stories." She could mesmerize any gathering, making people laugh one minute and cry the next. Tall and striking, Hurston was a flamboyant figure, with bangles and beads and always a hat.

"Zora stories" about her outrageous actions began circulating. Once, wearing a flowing white dress and heading out to a party, she punched a man who tried to embrace her in the elevator—and didn't look back as she left him lying on the floor. Another time she took a coin from the cup of a beggar, promising to repay him later, swearing that right now she needed this subway fare more than he did. Her bare Manhattan apartment was furnished by friends within days after her arrival in the city. Visitors contributed to the pot of stew on the stove; sometimes

Hurston cooked eel or fried okra. She would have everyone singing spirituals or playing drums while she played harmonica. But despite the noise and frivolity, she was serious about her writing: "I shall wrassle me up a future, or die trying."

She traveled to remote areas to gather material. A single woman traveling alone, she faced adventures small (bedbugs) and great (the worst hurricane to hit the Bahamas in years), as well as incidents that made her start carrying a revolver. She learned voodoo practices, photographed zombies (bodies supposedly called back from the dead), and became friends with a Jamaican medicine man who could quiet thousands of frogs. Once in New Orleans she had to pass a test to gain the trust of a Creole conjurer: lying naked face down on a couch for sixty-nine hours, without food or water, with a snakeskin touching her navel.

Hurston wrote on a card table in the cabins she rented and on her houseboat, the only property she ever owned. She was never wealthy. On the day she found out she had sold her first book, her landlord evicted her for nonpayment of rent. Years later, on the same day one of her stories appeared in the *Saturday Evening Post,* she was discovered working as a maid.

She had two brief marriages; one was to a man fifteen years younger who later claimed she had hexed him with voodoo spells. But she never felt she met a man who wouldn't interfere with her writing, and the writing always won out in the end.

Hurston preferred not to dwell on the racial prejudice she faced all her life. Most humiliating was the time a white doctor hurried her into a laundry closet to examine her so his other patients wouldn't have to see her. She claimed to find such incidents astonishing rather than ugly: "How *can* any deny themselves the pleasure of my company?"

The worst event in her life was being charged with abuse of a ten-year-old white boy. The charges were quickly dismissed, but when a black court employee leaked the story to the press, Hurston felt betrayed. The publicity was such a nightmare that she contemplated suicide: "All that I have believed in has failed me."

It is thought that Hurston was fifty-nine years old when she died of heart disease in a county welfare home. She was buried in a bright pink gown.

Her grave, in a segregated cemetery, was unmarked until 1973, when Alice Walker (one of many writers influenced by Hurston) installed a granite marker that named her "A Genius of the South."

*B*OOKMARKS

•❖ Hurston was the leading authority of her time on African-American folklore. She worked on *Mules and Men* for years, traveling around Florida and Louisiana collecting tales (such as "How the Cat Got Nine Lives," "Why Women Always Take Advantage of Men," and Brer Rabbit stories), jokes, songs, and folk remedies. *Mules and Men* has been called the most skillfully written book in the field of folklore. Hurston declared that this folklore was not "as easy to collect as it sounds" because the best material came from areas where people were most shy of strangers.

•❖ *Their Eyes Were Watching God,* considered Hurston's greatest novel, was her attempt to "embalm" the feelings she had for a West Indian lover. In the novel, Tea Cake Woods is the only man who accepts the main character, Janie Crawford, as an equal. This and other works by Hurston were neglected for many years, but in 1977 the Modern Language Association named *Their Eyes Were Watching God* the out-of-print book most in demand. In its new editions, it has sold steadily and has been called "one of the main foundations of African-American literature."

THE PERFECT COMPANION

Langston Hughes

BORN IN JOPLIN, MISSOURI, 1902
DIED IN NEW YORK CITY, 1967

*American poet famous for work collected in such
volumes as* Shakespeare in Harlem, Montage of a Dream Deferred,
The Weary Blues, *and* The Dream Keeper

"CHILDREN SHOULD BE born without parents," Langston Hughes once said.

His own father went to live in Mexico and hardly ever saw his son. A bitter man, he hated American blacks, and Hughes, in turn, hated his father. His mother left him with his grandmother for long periods while she worked away from home. Hughes turned early to books; if people in books suffered, at least they did it "in beautiful language."

Later, working on a ship bound for Africa, Hughes was the only crew member who had a box of books with him. Suddenly, in a bold attempt to leave his troubled past behind, he decided to throw the whole box overboard. The only book he kept was Walt Whitman's *Leaves of Grass.*

All his life Hughes was known as "the perfect companion." He was handsome, thoughtful, kind, and made friends easily. He loved to gossip and joke, and he ended almost every sentence with a chuckle. As sociable as Hughes was, though, there was always a part of himself that he kept private, and he reminded some people of a monk. (He never married, although several women proposed to him. Many people assumed he was homosexual, but the facts remain unknown.) He was a bad dancer, couldn't play a musical instrument, and his singing could scare people. But he loved blues and jazz music; his favorite song was Billie Holiday's "God Bless the Child That's Got His Own."

Hughes spent the first half of his life in "solitary wandering," staying with friends or renting rooms. Later, he lived in Harlem, New York, with the Harpers, a couple whom he thought of as an aunt and uncle. His two-room suite on the third floor of the house looked more like an office than a place to live. With different kinds of paper for each project, his desk was like a "Joseph's coat" of many colors. Hughes was never rich, but in 1959 was proud to "have lived longer than any other known Negro *solely* on writing—from 1925 to now without a regular job!!!!!"

Hughes got up at noon and started chain-smoking Camel cigarettes. After a large breakfast made by his "Aunt Toy" (he loved to eat and was often called a "roly-poly guy"), he dressed in a striped sailor's jersey. He wrote letters or met with visitors, feeding them cider and cake. He went out at night (often to the Baby Grand, his favorite club) and came back at 1:00 or 2:00 A.M., settling down to write as everyone else slept.

Hughes grew up in mostly white neighborhoods, where he faced everything from racist insults to physical attacks. His way of dealing with the constant racial prejudice was to leave a scene in quiet disgust or to write an angry letter afterward. His worst experience was in Atlanta, where he was stranded at the airport for hours because no taxi would accept a black passenger. He valued staying in control, and so he disliked confrontation (although once, when he was mugged, he fought back and took the attacker's weapon away). Sometimes there were bomb threats at his poetry readings, and at least one teacher was fired for reading a Hughes poem to his class. The FBI kept an elaborate file on him, full of information that was mostly false.

Hughes died at age sixty-five from complications of cancer-related surgery. He had requested that the music at his memorial service include W. C. Handy's "St. Louis Blues" and Duke Ellington's "Do Nothing Till You Hear from Me." People attending the service weren't sure whether to dance or act solemn, and they decided that Hughes was playing one last joke on all of them.

ℬOOKMARKS

➥ Unhappy and anxious, Hughes wrote "The Negro Speaks of Rivers," his first important poem, as a teenager on the train to make what turned out to be his last visit to his father. He began his autobiography, *The Big Sea,* on a train. On another train ride, to soothe himself after an experience so terrifying it had made him tremble (testifying before a Senate committee about his political views), he read Emily Dickinson. Though he clearly found inspiration on solitary train rides, Hughes later preferred to take planes because there were fewer problems with segregation.

➥ Hughes's favorite of his own books was *Dear Lovely Death.* Always fascinated by death, as a child he once ran away and spent the night in a local morgue.

➥ Dr. Martin Luther King, Jr., the civil rights leader, sometimes used Hughes's poems in his speeches. There are similarities between King's famous "I Have a Dream" speech and Hughes's poems, which refer often to dreams. *A Raisin in the Sun,* the first Broadway play by a black woman playwright (Lorraine Hansberry), took its title from Hughes's poem "Montage of a Dream Deferred."

Isaac Bashevis Singer

BORN IN LEONCIN, POLAND, 1904
DIED IN MIAMI, FLORIDA, 1991

*American writer of novels, short stories,
and children's books—considered one
of the world's great storytellers*

AS A CHILD in the Jewish ghetto of Warsaw, Poland, Icek-Herz Zynger studied the Jewish religion all day long at *cheder* (elementary school). His family was so poor — at times starving — that sometimes his only toy was a dried palm branch, and he would play with it for days. Reading outside of school made him forget his physical discomforts, especially after he discovered the tales of Edgar Allan Poe.

But the rise of anti-Jewish feeling in Europe sometimes gave him thoughts of suicide. At age thirty-one, by then known as Isaac Bashevis Singer (Bashevis is a variation on his mother's name, Bathsheba), he came to the United States. His first wife, Runya, and their son, Israel, moved to Russia and eventually to Palestine. They all escaped the Holocaust, when most Polish Jews, including some of Singer's family and friends, were killed by Nazis during World War II. All the places Singer had known in Poland were destroyed in the war; the world of his childhood was gone.

Singer began to re-create that old world in stories. He wrote in Yiddish (a mixture of German, Russian, and Slavic, written in Hebrew letters from right to left).

He typed on a rickety Yiddish-character typewriter and helped translators convert the stories into English. He wrote articles for *The Jewish Daily Forward,* a New York paper that also published installments of his stories. "I have to force myself *not* to write," he admitted.

Singer was devastated by the death of his adored older brother, Israel Joshua, a well-known writer. Yet his grief drove him to work harder, and his next book, *The Family Moskat,* was the one that brought fame.

Singer was married to his second wife, Alma, for fifty-one years. She worked for Saks Fifth Avenue department store and supported both of them until his writing started to bring in money. They divided their time between an apartment in Manhattan and a condominium in south Florida.

Singer got up every morning at eight o'clock, had cereal and a grapefruit or apple, and then sometimes went back to bed, where he wrote notes in inexpensive lined notebooks. In the afternoons he took long walks, sometimes to the *Forward* office to deliver stories or to a cafeteria to meet old friends (they called him Bashevis). He seldom watched TV or went to movies and didn't own a phonograph (so he never heard any of the recordings made of his stories).

He owned parakeets that flew free and sometimes landed on his bald head, and his neighbors knew him as someone who kept the pigeons well fed. He stopped eating meat out of his concern for animals. He wasn't a strict vegetarian, though; he ate eggs and did love blintzes stuffed with cheese.

Though he was still unknown at age forty, Singer eventually became famous and wealthy. But even then he lived simply; he was eating in a neighborhood drugstore when he learned he had won the Nobel Prize in literature. On the plane to receive his award, he read about himself in *People* magazine.

Pale and bald, Singer was the first to say he resembled an imp from one of his own stories. He wore dark suits, white shirts, and plain ties. He seemed frail, but

he moved with the speed of a chipmunk. To entertain children, he was known to run around the house barking like a dog.

He died at age eighty-seven after a stroke.

$\mathscr{B}$OOKMARKS

➽ Sometimes Singer's writing made people uncomfortable because it didn't always present a positive picture of Polish Jews, but many people think that he wrote the greatest short stories of our time. Some consider his best story to be "Gimpel the Fool" (translated by American writer Saul Bellow), about a gullible baker.

➽ Singer was sixty-two years old when he started writing children's books. Three of them were named by the American Library Association as Newbery Honor books—*Zlateh the Goat and Other Stories, The Fearsome Inn,* and *When Shlemiel Went to Warsaw and Other Stories.*

➽ Singer was usually unhappy with the way the movies of his works turned out; they didn't stick closely enough to his stories. Movies of his books include *Enemies, A Love Story* (which has many autobiographical elements), *Yentl* (starring Barbra Streisand), and *The Magician of Lublin* (starring Alan Arkin).

➽ To explain why he wrote in Yiddish, a language not many people know anymore, Singer said, "I like to write ghost stories, and nothing fits a ghost better than a dying language."

LITERARY TERMS

anonymous	giving no name as the author of a work
character	a person in a literary work
comedy	a literary work intended to amuse
edit	to change or refine a writer's work
editor	someone who edits for a living
essay	a brief prose work that addresses a particular subject
fiction	an invented story, as opposed to straight facts or nonfiction
folklore	legends, beliefs, etc. passed through generations by word of mouth
hero/heroine	the principal male or female character in a literary work
novel	a long work of fiction in prose (not poetry)
pen name	a pseudonym, or invented name, taken by a writer
plagiarism	an act of stealing and passing off another's work as one's own
play	a story meant to be performed by actors on stage
playwright	someone who writes plays
poem	a literary work in verse
publish	to produce a literary work in print
refrain	a line or lines repeated during the course of a poem
review	an evaluation, or criticism, of a literary work
revision	the result of rewriting a work in order to improve it
short story	a brief work of fiction in prose
sonnet	a poem in fourteen lines following strict rules of rhyme and rhythm
title page	the page of a book showing the title and the author
tragedy	a serious literary work with an unhappy ending
translate	to turn a work into one's own or another language
trilogy	a series of three related works
verse	lines of rhymed or rhythmic writing

ℐNDEX OF 𝒲RITERS

$\mathcal{F}$OR FURTHER READING . . . AND WRITING

Ackroyd, Peter. *Dickens*. New York: HarperCollins, 1990.

Barth, Edna. *I'm Nobody! Who Are You?: The Story of Emily Dickinson*. New York: Clarion, 1971.

Bowring, Richard, trans. *Murasaki Shikibu: Her Diary and Poetic Memoirs*. Princeton, New Jersey: Princeton University Press, 1982.

Calder, Jenni. *Robert Louis Stevenson: A Critical Celebration*. Totowa, New Jersey: Barnes & Noble Books, 1980.

Chute, Marchette. *Shakespeare of London*. New York: Dutton, 1949.

Fraser, Rebecca. *The Brontës: Charlotte Brontë and Her Family*. New York: Crown, 1988.

Gherman, Beverly. *E. B. White: Some Writer!* New York: Atheneum, 1992.

Honan, Park. *Jane Austen: Her Life*. New York: St. Martin's, 1987.

Johnston, Norma. *Louisa May: The World and Works of Louisa May Alcott*. New York: Four Winds, 1991.

Kresh, Paul. *Isaac Bashevis Singer: The Story of a Storyteller*. New York: Lodestar, 1984.

Lyons, Mary E. *Sorrow's Kitchen: The Life and Folklore of Zora Neale Hurston*. New York: Scribners, 1991.

McKendrick, Melveena. *Cervantes*. Boston: Little, Brown, 1980.

Meltzer, Milton. *Mark Twain: A Writer's Life*. New York: Watts, 1985.

Niven, Penelope. *Carl Sandburg: A Biography*. New York: Scribners, 1991.

Rampersad, Arnold. *The Life of Langston Hughes*. New York: Oxford University Press, 1986 (Volume I) and 1988 (Volume II).

Silverman, Kenneth. *Edgar A. Poe: Mournful and Never-Ending Remembrance*. New York: HarperCollins, 1991.

Stirling, Monica. *The Wild Swan: The Life and Times of Hans Christian Andersen*. New York: Harcourt Brace, 1965.

Thwaite, Ann. *Waiting for the Party: The Life of Frances Hodgson Burnett*. New York: Scribners, 1974.

. . . and books by the writers in this book